Faith and Resilience

The Lives of Jonathan Roumie and Takashi Nagai

Erikson Brown

Copyright © 2025 EriksonBrown.

All rights reserved. A written permission from the author is mandatory before anyone duplicates, distributes or transmits the content of this book through any form or method including photocopying, recording and mechanical or electronic ways except for brief quotations embedded in critical reviews and other authorized noncommercial uses allowed by copyright law.

Disclaimer

The book presents factual information derived from the actual lives of Jonathan Roumie and Takashi Nagai. The author made great strides in verifying all presented data yet specific points potentially needed interpretation to achieve narrative clarity. This book presents the author's points of view because the thoughts do not represent Jonathan Roumie nor Takashi Nagai nor their family members nor organizations that they work with.

Table of content

Introduction
- religion and Resilience throughout Time and Cultures

CHAPTER 1
- the adventure to faith – Jonathan Roumie's adolescence and career
- spiritual Awakening and give up to faith

CHAPTER 2
- the road to Nagasaki – Takashi Nagai's direction to religion

CHAPTER 3
- Portraying Christ – How Jonathan Roumie determined energy in religion

CHAPTER 4
- facing the Bomb – Takashi Nagai's Witness to Destruction

CHAPTER 5
- Resilience thru faith – How each men stimulated Others

CHAPTER 6
- classes in faith and Forgiveness

CHAPTER 7

- faith in action – persevering with Their Legacy

conclusion – United through faith and Resilience

Introduction

religion and Resilience throughout Time and Cultures

faith and resilience are two of the most effective forces that form human existence. throughout cultures, generations, and historic eras, individuals have determined power and purpose via their religious convictions and their ability to withstand existence's maximum difficult situations. faith gives a sense of which means and desire, whilst resilience enables individuals to stand adversity with braveness and perseverance. The lives of Jonathan Roumie and Takashi Nagai exemplify this profound connection among faith and resilience, demonstrating how spiritual conviction and internal power can manual humans through both non-public and collective trials.

Jonathan Roumie, a contemporary actor first-class acknowledged for his portrayal of Jesus Christ inside the selected, and Takashi Nagai, a Catholic health practitioner and radiologist who survived the atomic bombing of Nagasaki, come from massively distinct backgrounds and lived in exceptional historic durations. but, each guys embody a shared narrative of faith and resilience, using their private journeys to encourage and uplift others. Roumie's rise to prominence through his position within the chosen displays a adventure of non secular discovery and inventive determination, at the same time as Nagai's survival and non secular reaction to the destruction of Nagasaki highlight the power of forgiveness and peace within the face of inconceivable loss.

The lives of those figures serve as a powerful exploration of how religion and resilience go beyond time and way of life. notwithstanding their different contexts — Roumie inside the entertainment industry and Nagai in the aftermath of battle — each guys display that genuine energy comes now not from averting struggling, however from embracing it with faith and a willingness to heal. Their testimonies screen that resilience isn't sincerely approximately enduring hardship, however about locating a deeper cause within it and permitting religion to transform personal trials into acts of service and thought.

religion has continually played a principal function in human history, shaping societies, inspiring actions, and imparting solace in times of misery. throughout extraordinary religious traditions, faith is often visible as a guiding pressure that offers moral direction and emotional strength. For Jonathan Roumie, faith have become each a personal and expert anchor. Raised in a Catholic own family, Roumie's journey in the direction of deepening his religion was now not trustworthy. Like many artists, he struggled with economic instability and uncertainty in his profession. however, his non secular beliefs became more profound whilst he turned into cast as Jesus Christ in the selected.

Roumie has often spoken about how portraying Jesus required him to lean on his faith in methods he had by no means predicted. The obligation of depicting Christ's teachings and the emotional intensity of his sacrifice compelled Roumie to confront his personal non secular questions and weaknesses. via prayer and mirrored image, Roumie located strength inside the teachings of Christ, which no longer most effective encouraged his performance but additionally deepened his expertise of his non-public religion. Takashi Nagai's journey toward religion, however, became fashioned with the aid of a one-of-a-kind set of situations. Born right into a Shinto and Buddhist own family in Japan, Nagai to start with approached faith with skepticism. His conversion to Catholicism came through his publicity to Christian teachings and his courting with Midori Moriyama, a religious Catholic who could later emerge as his wife. Nagai's embody of Catholicism deepened his expertise of human struggling and redemption — lessons that might take on profound significance after the atomic bombing of Nagasaki in 1945.

Resilience is often defined because the capacity to withstand and get over trouble. while some humans may additionally view resilience as an individual trait, the lives of Roumie and Nagai show that authentic resilience is frequently tied to religion. The strength to bear struggling and locate meaning in it stems from the notion that there's a higher purpose beyond instantaneous ache.

Jonathan Roumie's resilience was tested through his early struggles as an actor. He faced years of rejection and financial instability, wondering his profession direction and his feel of cause. but, it become his faith that sustained him at some stage in those difficult instances. Roumie has spoken about moments when he prayed for steerage and power, finding peace inside the belief that his life had a extra motive. The fulfillment of the chosen turned into no longer definitely a career leap forward for Roumie; it became a spiritual calling that affirmed the connection between his faith and his artistic work.

Takashi Nagai's resilience, through assessment, became solid inside the crucible of battle and destruction. whilst the atomic bomb turned into dropped on Nagasaki on August nine, 1945,

Nagai witnessed the immediately devastation and the awful aftermath. He misplaced his spouse Midori inside the bombing and suffered from severe radiation exposure himself. no matter the vast non-public loss and bodily suffering, Nagai answered with superb grace and forgiveness. rather than succumbing to depression, he became to his religion for power, advocating for peace and reconciliation.

Nagai's writings and speeches after the bombing replicate a profound expertise of human struggling and the transformative strength of religion. In his well-known paintings The Bells of Nagasaki, Nagai defined how the destruction of the city turned into now not definitely a tragedy, however additionally an opportunity for spiritual rebirth. He referred to as on survivors to embrace forgiveness rather than hatred, framing the devastation as a route towards healing and peace. His resilience was not just about non-public survival, however about offering desire to others and guiding his network toward healing.

religion and Resilience as a supply of proposal

both Roumie and Nagai have emerge as symbols of religion and resilience of their respective fields. Roumie's portrayal of Jesus inside the selected has resonated deeply with audiences worldwide, imparting a fresh and emotionally wealthy depiction of Christ's teachings. His performance has inspired visitors to explore their personal faith trips, connecting with the humanity and compassion of Christ's message. Roumie's private testimony — how faith sustained him via career setbacks and moments of doubt — has made him a relatable determine for those navigating their personal non secular paths.

Nagai's legacy, then again, stays a supply of thought for the ones grappling with trauma and loss. His commitment to peace and forgiveness in the wake of not possible suffering continues to steer peace actions and religious discourse in Japan and beyond. Nagai's potential to locate meaning in the ruins of Nagasaki serves as a effective reminder that faith can remodel even the darkest moments into opportunities for recuperation and growth.

notwithstanding their one-of-a-kind backgrounds and life reviews, Jonathan Roumie and Takashi Nagai are united by a shared legacy of religion and resilience. Roumie's success in portraying Christ and Nagai's spiritual reaction to the bombing of Nagasaki each replicate the energy of faith to sustain and transform lives. Their tales underscore the prevalent nature of faith and resilience, demonstrating that real power comes now not from heading off suffering however from embracing it with consider in a higher motive.

Their lives project current believers to mirror on their own assets of power and faith. Roumie's adventure indicates that religion can guide inventive expression and personal success, at the same time as Nagai's tale reminds us that forgiveness and peace are viable even within the aftermath of profound destruction. together, their testimonies form a effective testament to the enduring connection among faith and resilience — a connection that transcends time, way of life, and situation.

faith and resilience are not summary ideas — they're lived reviews that form character lives and communities. Jonathan Roumie and Takashi Nagai stand as profound examples of ways faith can offer energy in the face of complication and how resilience can turn suffering into a supply of proposal and recuperation. Their trips monitor that even within the face of personal and collective tragedies, religion gives a path toward hope and peace. Their lives preserve to inspire others to trust in the transformative strength of faith and to stand lifestyles's demanding situations with braveness and charm.

CHAPTER 1

the adventure to faith – Jonathan Roumie's adolescence and career

faith is rarely a honest route. It frequently winds through uncertainty, non-public struggles, and surprising breakthroughs. For Jonathan Roumie, the adventure to faith was in detail tied to his non-public and expert lifestyles, fashioned by using early demanding situations, setbacks in his profession, and a profound non secular awakening that could subsequently outline his lifestyles's cause. Roumie's upward thrust to prominence thru his portrayal of Jesus Christ in the chosen was now not in reality a result of inventive expertise — it changed into a spiritual calling that emerged from years of personal mirrored image and perseverance. His story illustrates how religion and resilience are often forged within the crucible of adversity and the way trusting in a better purpose can transform life's most difficult moments into profound non secular growth.

Jonathan Roumie changed into born on July 1, 1974, in new york town to a multicultural and religiously numerous family. His father, a Catholic from Egypt with Syrian ancestry, and his mother, an Irish Catholic, raised him in the framework of the Catholic religion. Roumie grew up immersed in religious way of life, attending Mass frequently and participating in church lifestyles.

His upbringing was shaped by both the wealthy non secular background of the japanese Catholic Church and the extra established traditions of the Roman Catholic religion. This mixture of religious and cultural influences gave Roumie a wide attitude on spirituality from a younger age. His circle of relatives's commitment to faith laid the inspiration for his very own spiritual adventure, even though, like many younger humans, he would later conflict with questions of identity and motive.

Roumie displayed a herbal talent for the humanities from an early age. He become attracted to overall performance and storytelling, displaying an early interest in theater and film. After graduating from university, he decided to pursue a profession in acting — a path that might test his faith and resilience time and again.

Roumie's early years as an actor were marked by financial instability and professional rejection. He moved to l. a. to pursue his desires, however like many aspiring actors, he faced years of uncertainty and disappointment. He took on small roles in television and unbiased movies, however success remained elusive.

in the course of this era, Roumie regularly determined himself questioning his career desire and his cause. He faced moments of severe doubt, thinking if he had misunderstood his calling or if he become destined for failure. His financial struggles added to the pressure. At one point, Roumie become so broke that he couldn't come up with the money for lease or basic necessities. He later shared that there were moments whilst he had only some bucks left in his bank account and no clean route forward.

It became during these difficult instances that Roumie grew to become extra deeply to his faith. He recalled praying fervently, asking God for steerage and power. He began to embrace the idea that his lifestyles became no longer completely under his manipulate — that he needed to consider in God's plan even if the final results become uncertain. This surrender to faith marked a turning point in Roumie's non secular adventure.

spiritual Awakening and give up to faith

Roumie's step forward got here not via profession achievement however through spiritual give up. He described a moment when he knelt down in prayer and completely submitted his lifestyles to God. In that moment, he released his worry and anxiety, setting his agree with in God's plan as opposed to his personal efforts.

quickly after this non secular turning factor, Roumie acquired the opportunity that might alternate his existence. He become cast as Jesus Christ within the chosen, a multi-season tv series about the life of Jesus, created by means of Dallas Jenkins. The function changed into not really a professional possibility — it turned into a direct answer to the prayers Roumie had presented in the course of his darkest moments.

Roumie's coaching for the role of Jesus required more than just acting skill. He immersed himself in scripture and theological examine, looking for to understand the character of Christ on a deeper stage. He additionally deepened his very own prayer life, recognizing that portraying Jesus authentically required him to domesticate a non-public dating with God.

Roumie approached the position with humility and reverence. He regularly prayed before scenes, inquiring for the grace to mirror Christ's compassion, power, and humanity. He additionally leaned at the steering of non secular mentors and theologians, making sure that his portrayal remained authentic to the biblical narrative while shooting the emotional and human complexity of Jesus's lifestyles.

the chosen debuted in 2019 and speedy became a worldwide phenomenon. in contrast to traditional portrayals of Jesus, which regularly presented him in a distant or overly solemn manner, Roumie's depiction captured Christ's warm temperature, humor, and relatability. His performance resonated deeply with audiences, who responded not most effective to the show's creative satisfactory however additionally to the authenticity of Roumie's portrayal.

Roumie's non-public religion became intertwined together with his professional achievement. He regarded his role no longer truly as an acting activity, but as a spiritual challenge. He regularly spoke approximately how the show's achievement changed into an immediate mirrored image of God's work and how his own adventure closer to faith allowed him to connect with the individual of Jesus on a private stage.

one of the key moments in the selected that displays Roumie's intensity of religious expertise is the scene where Jesus calls Matthew the tax collector. Roumie's portrayal captures each the gentleness and authority of Christ, reflecting a deep internalization of Christ's message of mercy and redemption. Roumie later shared that this scene, and others adore it, required him to reflect on his very own reports of feeling misplaced and being called to a better cause.

Roumie's achievement in the chosen led to massive non-public and professional transformation. He have become a prominent parent within the Catholic and Christian communities, invited to speak at religion-based totally events and conferences. His testimony about his spiritual journey — such as the moments of doubt and surrender — stimulated audiences to reflect on their very own religion struggles.

Roumie also embraced the duty that came with portraying Christ. He diagnosed that his function made him a non secular ambassador of sorts, and he approached this duty with humility. He regularly reminded audiences that he turned into no longer perfect and that his portrayal of Jesus was rooted in his very own want for grace and forgiveness.

Roumie's career success did no longer separate him from his faith — it deepened it. He continued to rely on prayer and religious steerage as he navigated the pressures of repute and public scrutiny. He also used his platform to advocate for reasons aligned along with his faith, inclusive of social justice troubles and support for marginalized groups.

Jonathan Roumie's journey to religion illustrates numerous key classes about resilience and non secular growth. First, his tale shows that success often follows give up. Roumie's step forward got here now not when he attempted to control his profession, however whilst he surrendered it to God. 2d, his experience highlights the importance of authenticity in religion. Roumie's ability to painting Christ authentically stemmed from his personal dedication to dwelling out Christ's teachings in his private existence.

eventually, Roumie's tale reminds us that religion isn't always about warding off conflict, however about finding strength within it. His early years of professional and monetary difficulty shaped his person and deepened his reliance on God. This resilience allowed him to technique his function within the chosen with the emotional depth and non secular adulthood required to authentically reflect Christ's message.

Jonathan Roumie's journey to religion and professional achievement displays the profound connection among faith and resilience. His tale demonstrates that authentic electricity comes no longer from personal attempt on my own, but from a willingness to give up to God's plan and consider in His steerage. Roumie's portrayal of Jesus within the selected is greater than a performance — it is a mirrored image of his own spiritual adventure and the transformative power of faith. His lifestyles serves as a testomony to the concept that religion and resilience aren't separate forces however interconnected factors that shape and preserve a existence rooted in purpose and trust in God.

CHAPTER 2

the road to Nagasaki – Takashi Nagai's direction to religion

faith is regularly discovered no longer in moments of comfort, however within the depths of suffering and existential questioning. The lifestyles of Takashi Nagai, a jap health practitioner and radiologist who survived the atomic bombing of Nagasaki, illustrates how faith can emerge from non-public tragedy and highbrow searching. Nagai's direction to religion was now not direct — it was marked by using medical skepticism, philosophical inquiry, and private loss. however, his eventual conversion to Catholicism and his profound reaction to the devastation of Nagasaki mirror the transformative power of religion and resilience. Nagai's adventure well-knownshows that faith isn't always merely a depend of perception, but a profound internal transformation that permits a person to confront even the maximum unattainable suffering with grace and forgiveness. Takashi Nagai changed into born on February 3, 1908, in the city of Matsue, within the Shimane Prefecture of Japan. He turned into raised in a Shinto and Buddhist household, which meditated the conventional non secular history of jap society. His father, a scientific medical doctor, endorsed Takashi's interest in technology and medicine from an early age. Nagai's academic brilliance soon have become glaring, and he decided to pursue a career in medication.

In 1928, Nagai enrolled at Nagasaki scientific university (now Nagasaki college), where he studied medicinal drug with a focus on radiology. He was deeply inspired through the rise of modern-day medical questioning and rationalism. Like many young intellectuals of his time, Nagai became skeptical of faith, viewing it as a relic of a pre-medical technology. His medical schooling led him to consider that human lifestyles might be defined entirely thru bodily and organic techniques.

but, Nagai's rationalist worldview started to resolve as he confronted deeper questions about life, death, and human struggling. His paintings in radiology exposed him to the fragility of the human body, at the same time as his growing cognizance of the political and social instability in pre-war Japan forced him to don't forget the ethical and spiritual dimensions of life. It became at some point of this era of highbrow looking that Nagai encountered the Catholic faith thru an sudden supply — a young woman named Midori Moriyama.

Midori Moriyama became a devout Catholic, a rarity in a country where much less than one percent of the populace practiced Christianity. Midori came from a Catholic family with deep roots in Nagasaki's Christian community — a network that had suffered centuries of persecution under Japan's anti-Christian laws. despite the suppression of Christianity, Nagasaki had remained a stronghold of japanese Catholicism.

Nagai met Midori whilst he become running as a scientific pupil. Her quiet faith and internal power impressed him. Midori's notion in God and her commitment to prayer and moral integrity challenged Nagai's rationalist worldview. He started to impeach whether technological know-how by myself may want to provide solutions to existence's most profound questions.

at some stage in a Christmas Eve Mass at Urakami Cathedral, Midori invited Nagai to wait the provider. Nagai was moved by way of the beauty and solemnity of the Mass, in particular the feel of peace and wish that the congregation appeared to encompass. It was a stark assessment to the growing militarism and political unrest in Japan.

Nagai's highbrow war with faith reached a turning point while Midori gave him a copy of The Confessions via St. Augustine. Nagai became struck by Augustine's journey from skepticism to faith, spotting parallels along with his own look for reality. Augustine's exploration of purpose and notion resonated deeply with Nagai's clinical thoughts and philosophical doubts.

inspired by way of Midori's example and Augustine's writings, Nagai started to discover

Catholic teachings extra seriously. He studied scripture, attended Mass, and sought guidance from Catholic monks in Nagasaki. through the years, his skepticism gave manner to a growing sense of religious conviction. He got here to look science and faith no longer as opposing forces, however as complementary paths to understanding human existence.

In 1934, Nagai made the decision to be baptized into the Catholic Church. He took the Christian call Paul, in honor of St. Paul's very own dramatic conversion from skepticism to religion. His baptism become not merely a proper announcement of perception — it represented a profound shift in Nagai's worldview. He now viewed his paintings as a health practitioner now not handiest as a systematic career however as a spiritual vocation.

Nagai's faith changed into soon tested by using personal and expert demanding situations. He married Midori in 1934, and that they started to construct a circle of relatives collectively. however, Nagai's work as a radiologist uncovered him to high ranges of radiation, and he started to be afflicted by the early signs and symptoms of radiation sickness. despite his declining fitness, he continued his scientific work, viewing his struggling as a manner to unite himself with the redemptive suffering of Christ.

in the course of the outbreak of worldwide battle II, Nagai served as a army physician, treating wounded infantrymen and witnessing the devastating outcomes of struggle firsthand. His religion deepened as he faced the ethical and moral questions posed by means of conflict and human struggling. He often became to prayer and the lessons of Christ for steerage, finding solace in the message of peace and forgiveness.

August 9, 1945 – The Atomic Bombing of Nagasaki

Nagai's faith would face its greatest test on August nine, 1945, whilst the us dropped an atomic bomb on Nagasaki. Nagai turned into running at Nagasaki scientific university when the bomb detonated over the metropolis. The blast killed tens of heaps of human beings immediately and decreased lots of the metropolis to rubble.

Midori changed into at domestic whilst the bomb struck, and Nagai's worst fears had been found out while he discovered that she were killed. despite his personal injuries and the chaos surrounding him, Nagai immediately started treating survivors, the use of the confined medical materials to be had. He labored tirelessly within the days following the bombing, regardless of his worsening fitness.

within the midst of this devastation, Nagai's religion did not waver. as opposed to succumbing to depression or anger, he responded with forgiveness and compassion. He publicly declared that Nagasaki have been supplied as a sacrifice for peace, likening the town's suffering to the sacrifice of Christ on the cross. This theological interpretation of the bombing helped survivors discover meaning within the destruction and paved the way for reconciliation and restoration.

in the years after the bombing, Nagai have become a symbol of peace and non secular power.

He wrote considerably about his revel in and his belief that Nagasaki's suffering ought to serve as a catalyst for worldwide peace. His most well-known work, The Bells of Nagasaki, reflects his deep conviction that forgiveness, no longer revenge, became the course ahead.

Nagai's health persisted to decline due to radiation sickness. notwithstanding his physical weak point, he remained active in his scientific and non secular work. He installed a small network for orphans and survivors, offering medical care and emotional help. He also continued to speak publicly approximately the significance of forgiveness and peace.

On might also 1, 1951, Takashi Nagai died on the age of forty three. His dying marked the cease of a life defined through religion, carrier, and resilience. but, his legacy endures via his writings, the survivors he cared for, and the peace movement inspired by means of his message.

Takashi Nagai's path to faith teaches us that religious conviction isn't cut loose highbrow or medical inquiry — it regularly emerges thru it. His willingness to confront hard questions about life and dying led him to find out the deeper truths of Christian religion. His reaction to the atomic bombing of Nagasaki reminds us that resilience is not pretty much surviving suffering however approximately locating a higher meaning within it.

Nagai's life demanding situations us to do not forget how faith can rework not only person lives but also groups or even countries. His message of peace and forgiveness maintains to resonate in a world still grappling with conflict and department. via his example, Nagai reminds us that authentic power comes no longer from energy or manage, however from the potential to forgive and heal even within the face of profound loss.

Takashi Nagai's adventure to faith and resilience reflects the profound connection between non-public struggling and non secular transformation. His ability to respond to the devastation of Nagasaki with forgiveness and peace stands as a testament to the strength of religion to overcome even the darkest moments of human records. His existence maintains to encourage those looking for wish and restoration inside the aftermath of tragedy.

CHAPTER 3

Portraying Christ – How Jonathan Roumie determined energy in religion

Jonathan Roumie's portrayal of Jesus Christ inside the selected isn't only a innovative success — it is the culmination of a deeply and spiritual adventure. To step into the placement of Christ required greater than appearing capability; it demanded a profound religious connection, emotional vulnerability, and a willingness to give up to God's steering. Roumie's performance has resonated with tens of thousands and thousands of visitors global as it shows no longer most effective the ancient and theological components of Christ's lifestyles but additionally the personal, human side of Jesus — his compassion, electricity, and vulnerability. This chapter explores how Roumie's portrayal of Christ have emerge as a spiritual calling, how he prepared for the location, and the way his religion deepened thru the technique.

Jonathan Roumie's journey to portraying Jesus became not the cease end result of strategic profession planning — it emerged from an area of private give up and trust in God's plan. earlier than the chosen, Roumie had spent years suffering to locate regular art work as an actor. He had seemed in small roles in television and film, but his profession had stalled. Financially and emotionally, Roumie had reached a breaking factor.

He later shared that really before being forged inside the selected, he had $20 in his financial institution account and changed into unsure how he might pay his lease. In a second of desperation, Roumie knelt in prayer and surrendered his profession and destiny to God. He recollects announcing, "God, I surrender. i will't do this by myself anymore. I want you to take over." This prayer marked a turning point in Roumie's non secular lifestyles.

rapidly after this 2d of give up, Roumie received a call from Dallas Jenkins, the author and director of the selected. Jenkins had worked with Roumie previously on a brief movie wherein Roumie performed Jesus. Jenkins believed that Roumie's combination of heat, intensity, and authenticity made him the precise desire for the lead position in the selected, a multi-season series depicting the existence and ministry of Jesus.

Roumie's recognition of the position become now not in reality a profession decision — it felt like an answer to prayer. He appeared it as an instantaneous reaction to his act of give up and a affirmation that God had a plan for his life. Roumie knew that portraying Jesus would be a profound obligation — one that could require him to align his personal faith with his professional paintings.

Portraying Jesus required Roumie to interact in both intellectual and religious schooling. He immersed himself in scripture, reading the Gospels cautiously to apprehend the lessons and persona of Jesus. He consulted with biblical pupils and theologians to make sure that his portrayal remained dedicated to historic and theological accuracy.

but, Roumie knew that portraying Jesus authentically should require more than highbrow know-how — it'd require a deep qconnection to Christ's humanity and divinity. He deepened his private prayer lifestyles, spending time in Eucharistic adoration and attending Mass regularly. He additionally began praying the Divine Mercy Chaplet and the Rosary each day, looking for to align his coronary heart with Christ's message of mercy and forgiveness.

Roumie additionally fasted and practiced non secular disciplines to cultivate humility and non secular popularity. He diagnosed that portraying Jesus turn out to be now not approximately raising his very very own identification as an actor — it modified into about permitting Christ to paintings thru him. He frequently described himself as a vessel, searching out to mirror Christ's love and compassion in vicinity of his private interpretation of the character.

Emotionally, Roumie organized for the position by means of reflecting on his non-public reports of doubt, failure, and forgiveness. He recalled the moments while he had felt out of place and the way God's grace had guided him through the ones struggles. those personal reflections allowed Roumie to connect to the moments in Jesus's existence in which he professional rejection, betrayal, and suffering.
one of the defining factors of Roumie's portrayal inside the decided on is his functionality to seize the humanity of Christ. traditional portrayals of Jesus regularly gift him as faraway, solemn, or

emotionally detached. In assessment, Roumie's depiction famous a Christ who laughs, cries, jokes along with his disciples, and expresses real human emotion.

in one memorable scene from the number one season, Jesus calls Matthew the tax collector to comply with him. Matthew, considered a social outcast and a traitor thru his fellow Jews, hesitates in disbelief even as Jesus extends his invitation. Roumie's expression of warmth and truth in that 2d reflects not simplest the theological reality of Christ's ordinary call to sinners but moreover Roumie's private information of God's mercy.

Roumie's portrayal emphasizes Christ's relational nature — his ability to meet human beings in which they may be, to sincerely receive them without judgment, and to provide them a path to transformation. This aspect of the character resonated with Roumie's very own enjoy of feeling called out of expert failure and non secular doubt right right into a deeper dating with God.

every other key scene that displays Roumie's intensity of emotional know-how is the recovery of the leper. As Jesus tactics the leper, Roumie's facial expression reflects a mixture of compassion and authority. He touches the man or woman's face, a gesture that would were socially and religiously scandalous on the time. Roumie later defined that this second was inspired by using his non-public knowledge of Christ's radical compassion — the concept that Jesus meets human beings at their maximum damaged kingdom and heals them thru love and recognition.

Portraying Jesus got here with a vast quantity of stress and non secular war. Roumie frequently spoke about how he faced moments of self-doubt and non secular attack at some stage in filming. He defined experiencing unexplained tension and moments wherein he felt beaten by using way of the obligation of the position.

In reaction, Roumie leaned on prayer and the assist of his fellow solid and institution individuals. He might frequently pray with Dallas Jenkins and the producing institution in advance than filming hard scenes. He also sought religious course from priests and religion mentors, recognizing that portraying Christ authentically required him to stay spiritually grounded.

Roumie's capability to address the pressure of the position became rooted in his expertise that the fulfillment of the chosen changed into no longer ultimately his obligation — it grow to be God's. He taken into consideration himself as a vessel, trusting that God could work through him even supposing he felt insufficient or uncertain.

Roumie's portrayal of Jesus not most effective stimulated audiences international — it moreover deepened his non-private faith. He described the revel in of portraying Christ as a shape of non secular formation. by means of entering into the person of Jesus, Roumie gained a deeper facts of Christ's message of affection, forgiveness, and redemption.

Roumie regularly pondered on how portraying Jesus had changed his approach to relationships and personal traumatic situations. He became more affected man or woman, compassionate, and forgiving. He also grew greater assured in his prayer life, spotting that God's steerage and provision were constant despite the fact that activities regarded hard.

In interviews, Roumie shared that the maximum worthwhile part of his artwork on the chosen was hearing from visitors whose faith have been renewed or restored through the show. those who had left the church or struggled with private faith crises often shared that Roumie's portrayal of Christ had reminded them of God's love and mercy.

Jonathan Roumie's revel in of portraying Christ teaches several profound lessons about religion and resilience. First, his adventure reflects the energy of give up — his jump ahead came first-rate after he surrendered his career and destiny to God. second, his tale highlights the significance of authenticity in religion. Roumie's portrayal resonates as it presentations his private dating with Christ.

sooner or later, Roumie's revel in demonstrates that non secular electricity does no longer come from personal self warranty, but from reliance on God's grace. His capacity to address the strain and responsibility of portraying Christ stems from his know-how that God's power is made perfect in human weak spot.

Jonathan Roumie's portrayal of Jesus within the chosen is greater than an imaginative success — it's miles a sworn announcement to the transformative energy of faith and give up. His personal journey from expert failure to religious success mirrors the message of Christ's redemptive love. through his paintings, Roumie has no longer best added the story of Jesus to existence for tens of millions of viewers however additionally confirmed how faith and resilience can form a life of profound spiritual purpose.

CHAPTER 4

facing the Bomb – Takashi Nagai's Witness to Destruction

On August nine, 1945, at precisely 11:02 a.m., Takashi Nagai's lifestyles — along side the metropolis of Nagasaki — become modified for all time. The atomic bomb that detonated over Nagasaki decreased the town to ashes, killing tens of hundreds of people right away and leaving many extra to die from injuries and radiation exposure. Nagai, a physician and radiologist, turned into at the Nagasaki medical college while the bomb exploded. The event not best marked a turning factor in his personal existence but additionally have become a defining moment in his spiritual journey. confronted with the value of destruction and struggling, Nagai responded no longer with despair or bitterness, however with religion, forgiveness, and a name for peace. His movements within the aftermath of the bombing turned him into a symbol of resilience and spiritual strength, inspiring not most effective the survivors of Nagasaki however also a worldwide movement towards healing and reconciliation.

August nine, 1945, started out like any other day for Takashi Nagai. despite the continued struggle, he suggested to his submit at the Nagasaki medical university, wherein he served as a professor and a radiologist. Nagai turned into no stranger to suffering — years of working with radiation had weakened his body, and he become already showing signs of leukemia resulting from extended exposure to X-rays. but, Nagai remained committed to his work, viewing his clinical carrier as an extension of his faith and calling.

At eleven:02 a.m., Nagai changed into within the scientific university's radiology department when a dazzling flash of mild and an intense wave of warmth tore through the constructing. The blast become accompanied by way of a deafening roar and a effective shockwave that shattered home windows, collapsed walls, and threw Nagai throughout the room.

whilst Nagai regained focus, he found himself partially buried under the particles. His head turned into bleeding, and his frame become bruised, however he managed to drag himself free. As he emerged from the rubble, Nagai turned into faced with a vision of not possible destruction. The once-thriving town of Nagasaki turned into now a desolate tract of smoking ruins and scattered bodies. Fires burned across the city, and the air changed into packed with the cries of the wounded and dying.

Nagai later described the scene as a imaginative and prescient of hell. The Urakami district, which were the coronary heart of Nagasaki's Catholic community, lay in ruins. Urakami Cathedral, the largest Catholic church in East Asia, were completely destroyed. The trustworthy who had amassed there for morning Mass had been killed immediately.

Amid the chaos and destruction, Nagai's first thoughts became to his spouse, Midori. He knew that she have been at home in Urakami on the time of the bombing. regardless of his very own injuries, Nagai began making his way closer to their house, navigating via the burning wreckage and assisting wounded survivors alongside the way.

when he reached the website wherein their house had stood, he located handiest smoldering particles. After searching through the rubble, he observed Midori's rosary beads — a signal that she were praying whilst the bomb struck. sooner or later, he discovered her stays. Midori have been killed right away by the blast.

Nagai became devastated, however he become no longer triumph over by means of bitterness. He knelt beside Midori's frame and prayed, imparting her soul to God. He later contemplated that Midori's death changed into no longer meaningless — he believed that she had provided her lifestyles as a sacrifice for peace. Nagai took consolation in the fact that Midori had died in a country of prayer, retaining onto her faith even in her final moments.

regardless of his grief and injuries, Nagai straight away returned to his paintings as a physician. He joined a crew of surviving medical personnel at the Nagasaki medical university and started out treating the wounded. The situations had been terrible — the health center turned into critically damaged, medical elements were scarce, and the wide variety of injured beaten the body of workers.

Nagai dealt with sufferers with burns, damaged bones, and radiation sickness. He worked tirelessly for days without rest, the usage of his information in radiology to diagnose and deal with the effects of radiation exposure — while he himself commenced to suffer from the symptoms of radiation poisoning.

in the midst of this suffering, Nagai's religion did no longer falter. He advocated the survivors to pray and to are looking for energy in God. He reminded them that even in the face of destruction, they were not abandoned. His calm presence and quiet faith inspired those around him, giving them a sense of wish amid the devastation.

in the weeks and months following the bombing, Nagai commenced to mirror deeply on the which means of the destruction. even as many survivors were consumed with anger and bitterness closer to the usa and the japanese authorities, Nagai responded with a message of forgiveness and reconciliation.

In a public address, Nagai declared that Nagasaki were selected by way of God to suffer for the sake of peace. He as compared the city's destruction to the sacrifice of Christ at the cross, suggesting that Nagasaki's struggling could serve as a redemptive act for the sins of humanity.

This theological interpretation of the bombing became debatable, but it resonated with many survivors who were struggling to make feel of their suffering. Nagai's message of peace and forgiveness helped to prevent the outbreak of revenge and violence inside the aftermath of the attack. He encouraged survivors to rebuild their lives with faith and hope as opposed to hatred.

inside the years following the bombing, Nagai's fitness deteriorated due to radiation illness. in spite of his physical weakness, he endured to write and communicate publicly approximately the want for peace and forgiveness. His most famous work, The Bells of Nagasaki (Nagasaki no Kane), have become a image of Nagasaki's spiritual resilience.

in the Bells of Nagasaki, Nagai pondered on the bombing and its aftermath, focusing no longer on the political or navy implications however at the human and religious classes. He called for an stop to war and the promotion of peace thru forgiveness and reconciliation. He wrote that the sound of the bells of Urakami Cathedral, which had survived the bombing, represented the iconic presence of God's grace within the city.

Nagai additionally devoted his final years to rebuilding Nagasaki's Catholic network. He helped establish orphanages and care centers for survivors. He converted his own house into a place of prayer and reflection, where site visitors ought to are searching for spiritual healing.

As Nagai's health declined, he familiar his suffering with grace and religion. He regarded his infection as a form of participation in Christ's struggling. In his very last writings, he expressed gratitude for the possibility to witness to God's love even through ache and loss.

On can also 1, 1951, Takashi Nagai died at the age of forty three. His funeral changed into attended through thousands of Nagasaki's citizens, consisting of survivors of the bombing. His message of peace and forgiveness left a long-lasting impact on the town and past.

Nagai's life and witness continue to inspire peace moves and reconciliation efforts around the arena. His willingness to forgive and his capability to find that means in struggling mirror the transformative power of faith. His legacy serves as a reminder that even within the face of destruction, the human spirit can upward thrust thru forgiveness, wish, and resilience.

Takashi Nagai's reaction to the atomic bombing of Nagasaki teaches profound instructions about religion and resilience. First, his potential to forgive demonstrates that proper peace comes not from revenge however from reconciliation. 2nd, his determination to recovery survivors reflects the moral obligation to reply to suffering with compassion and carrier. subsequently, his theological interpretation of the bombing demanding situations us to are looking for that means in even the maximum tragic events.

via his existence and witness, Nagai reminds us that religion is not an break out from struggling — it is the electricity to face struggling with wish and braveness. His tale stands as a testament to the energy of faith to transform even the darkest moments of human records into opportunities for redemption and peace.

CHAPTER 5

Resilience thru faith – How each men stimulated Others

faith and resilience are often examined inside the face of profound struggling and uncertainty. For Jonathan Roumie and Takashi Nagai, faith turned into no longer merely a supply of private strength — it have become a guiding force that allowed them to inspire others and deliver hope to those grappling with their very own trials. in spite of dwelling in exclusive eras and under vastly exceptional occasions, Roumie and Nagai shared a commonplace reaction to adversity: they selected religion over depression, forgiveness over bitterness, and wish over worry. Their lives stand as powerful examples of ways faith can grow to be a wellspring of resilience, not handiest for oneself however additionally for the wider community.

Jonathan Roumie's rise to global recognition thru his portrayal of Jesus Christ inside the chosen is not only a story of creative achievement — it is an affidavit to the transformative energy of religion. Roumie's potential to inspire others stems from the authenticity of his personal religious journey and the manner he channels that religion into his work.

Roumie's portrayal of Jesus inside the chosen has touched tens of millions of viewers worldwide, reducing across spiritual, cultural, and generational divides. What sets his portrayal aside is the humanity he brings to the person of Christ. Audiences have replied now not handiest to the theological truth of his performance however also to the emotional intensity and vulnerability he conveys.

Roumie's model of Christ is approachable and compassionate, giggling along with his disciples, comforting the brokenhearted, and showing tenderness toward sinners. This depiction resonates with viewers who may additionally have formerly felt distanced from the parent of Jesus. for plenty, seeing a Christ who's emotionally gift and relational has renewed their religion and endorsed them to deepen their relationship with God.

Letters and tales have poured in from people who credit score the chosen with rekindling their spiritual lives. people who had left the Church or lost religion have shared that Roumie's portrayal helped them see Jesus now not as a far off theological parent but as a loving and available presence. Roumie himself has spoken about receiving messages from prisoners, addicts, and people suffering from intellectual infection who say that his portrayal of Christ gave them the courage to are looking for forgiveness and recuperation.

Roumie's effect extends beyond the display screen. His personal faith journey — including his selection to surrender his profession to God — has inspired others to agree with in God's plan even when instances seem hopeless. Roumie frequently stocks that his achievement inside the selected was the end result of God's intervention at a second when he changed into dealing with economic and professional failure.

via interviews, social media, and public speakme, Roumie encourages others to are looking for a private dating with Christ. He speaks openly approximately his reliance on prayer, the sacraments, and religious disciplines including fasting and Eucharistic adoration. His humility and willingness to percentage his struggles make his message relatable and on hand to a huge audience.

Roumie has extensively utilized his platform to propose for religious boom and social outreach. He companions with organizations that deal with poverty, dependancy, and intellectual fitness troubles, encouraging others to extend Christ's compassion via service. His message emphasizes that faith isn't simply a non-public experience — it is supposed to encourage motion and produce recovery to others.

Roumie's paintings has no longer been without controversy. some have criticized the chosen for its innovative liberties with the biblical narrative. Others have questioned Roumie's selection to take on the function of Jesus, arguing that depicting Christ on display screen carries theological dangers. Roumie has faced these challenges with grace and humility.

He always responds to criticism with a spirit of prayer and discernment. He has emphasised that his intention isn't to provide a definitive theological interpretation of Christ however to mirror the coronary heart of Christ's message — love, forgiveness, and redemption. Roumie's capacity to address public scrutiny without bitterness displays the energy of his private religion.

Takashi Nagai's legacy as a health practitioner, survivor of the Nagasaki bombing, and advise for peace keeps to inspire humans around the arena. His capability to transform non-public suffering into a message of forgiveness and wish made him a spiritual beacon within the aftermath of the atomic bombing.

in the on the spot aftermath of the Nagasaki bombing, many survivors had been fed on with anger and bitterness closer to america and the japanese government. Nagai's response became radically specific — he preached forgiveness.

Nagai interpreted the destruction of Nagasaki now not as a punishment however as a call to religious renewal. He publicly declared that Nagasaki have been chosen to bear the load of this suffering so that peace may be born from its ashes. His willingness to forgive the perpetrators of the bombing turned into not naïve — it was a deliberate act of religion.

Nagai's message of forgiveness gave survivors a route closer to recovery. instead of looking for revenge, they were advocated to rebuild their lives with a focal point on reconciliation and peace. Nagai reminded his fellow survivors that Christ's sacrifice on the go confirmed that forgiveness is the ultimate path to spiritual freedom.

Nagai's private life reflected the message he preached. After the bombing, he selected no longer to leave Nagasaki no matter his declining health. He continued to treat radiation victims at the same time as his very own frame weakened. He donated a great deal of his earnings from The Bells of Nagasaki to assist rebuild the Catholic network in Urakami.

Nagai's residence have become a domain of pilgrimage, in which survivors and site visitors from around the world came to searching for non secular guidance. even if he became bedridden in his final months, Nagai continued to write letters and provide prayers for those in want.

His capability to serve others notwithstanding his own suffering have become a model of Christian sacrifice. Survivors often defined Nagai as a living embodiment of Christ's message: "more love has no person than this, that someone lay down his existence for his friends" (John 15:thirteen).

Nagai's legacy extends past Nagasaki. His writings, specially The Bells of Nagasaki, were translated into more than one languages and have inspired peace moves around the sector. His message that authentic peace requires both forgiveness and justice keeps to resonate in global dialogues approximately warfare and reconciliation.

Nagai's tale has also stimulated artists, filmmakers, and historians to mirror on the moral classes of nuclear war. His willingness to speak about the human cost of the bombing — without bitterness or political condemnation — remains a effective name for ethical responsibility and peace.

though separated by means of time, geography, and circumstance, Jonathan Roumie and Takashi Nagai percentage a common spiritual legacy. each men validated that faith isn't always passive — it is an lively pressure that transforms individuals and communities.

Roumie's portrayal of Christ reminds visitors that faith is relational — Christ's invitation to follow him is an invite to transformation and healing. Nagai's response to the bombing of Nagasaki reflects that faith isn't always weakened by using struggling — it's far strengthened whilst struggling is obtainable as a sacrifice for others.

both guys inspire others to reply to adversity with faith instead of worry. Roumie's work challenges viewers to encounter Christ for my part, even as Nagai's witness challenges humanity to are looking for peace thru forgiveness. Their lives display that faith is not simplest a source of personal energy — it is a course to healing and renewal for the whole human family.

Jonathan Roumie and Takashi Nagai train us that authentic resilience comes no longer from human power however from believe in God's plan. Roumie's ability to reflect Christ's compassion through his art and Nagai's willingness to forgive inside the face of not possible suffering reveal that faith is a source of both personal recuperation and collective transformation. Their testimonies remind us that faith, whilst truely lived, will become a source of mild even inside the darkest of times.

CHAPTER 6

classes in faith and Forgiveness

faith and forgiveness are a few of the most powerful forces that form human enjoy. They offer power inside the face of adversity, healing inside the aftermath of trauma, and the potential to transform not only man or woman lives however entire communities. The tales of Jonathan Roumie and Takashi Nagai provide profound classes in how religion and forgiveness can end up resources of resilience, braveness, and renewal. in spite of living in distinct eras and dealing with hugely distinct demanding situations, each men verified that genuine religion isn't always passive — it's miles an energetic pressure that empowers human beings to confront suffering with grace and to respond to injustice with mercy. Their lives function powerful reminders that forgiveness isn't a signal of weak spot however a testomony to religious energy.

This chapter explores the important thing training in faith and forgiveness drawn from the lives of Jonathan Roumie and Takashi Nagai. Their testimonies display that forgiveness is not simply an emotional launch — it's miles a aware act of religion that transforms the person that forgives and creates the muse for peace and reconciliation. Likewise, religion isn't always simply a source of comfort; it's far the strength that allows individuals to confront life's private demanding situations with braveness and reason.

Jonathan Roumie's journey to religion was fashioned through moments of uncertainty and failure. before his achievement with the chosen, Roumie confronted a length of economic instability and expert frustration. despite years of difficult work and willpower, his appearing career had not materialized as he had was hoping. He become all the way down to his closing greenbacks and thinking whether or not he had misunderstood his calling.

In a second of desperation, Roumie fell to his knees and surrendered his future to God. He prayed, asking God to take control of his lifestyles and career. shortly afterward, he become forged as Jesus inside the chosen, a function that could no longer most effective remodel his career however also his faith.

Roumie's tale teaches that genuine religion requires give up. while Roumie chose to believe in God's plan instead of depend upon his own expertise, he experienced a step forward that surpassed his expectations. His success in the selected become not genuinely a career victory — it became a spiritual challenge, allowing him to use his platform to carry others in the direction of Christ.

The lesson right here is that faith isn't simply about notion — it's miles approximately trust. Roumie's willingness to place his destiny in God's hands displays the essence of Christian faith: agree with that God's plan is extra than human understanding, even when the path ahead appears doubtful.

Takashi Nagai's religion changed into forged through struggling. As a clinical scholar, Nagai changed into delivered to Christianity via the Catholic faith of his future spouse, Midori. no matter preliminary skepticism, he became drawn to the teachings of Christ, specifically the message of sacrificial love. His conversion to Catholicism marked the beginning of a faith adventure that could be tested under the most excessive circumstances.

The atomic bombing of Nagasaki destroyed Nagai's home and took the life of his spouse. but, as opposed to succumbing to despair, Nagai replied with faith. He interpreted the bombing as a name for non secular renewal and forgiveness. His willingness to serve the wounded and his choice to forgive the ones answerable for the bombing contemplated a deep agree with in God's providence.

Nagai's religion teaches that notion in God does now not guard us from suffering — but it gives us the energy to stand it. His story demanding situations the belief that religion is only significant whilst lifestyles is comfy. rather,

Nagai's life demonstrates that faith reaches its fullest expression while it enables us to face suffering with braveness and compassion.

As an actor portraying Jesus, Roumie consists of the duty of embodying Christ's message of forgiveness. in the chosen, Christ's interactions with sinners, outcasts, and the brokenhearted replicate the heart of Christian forgiveness — unconditional reputation and charm.

Roumie's capability to deliver Christ's forgiveness on display has had a profound impact on viewers. Many have shared that seeing Jesus' compassion for the tax collector Matthew or his willingness to heal the leper helped them recognize God's mercy in a private way. a few have even credited Roumie's portrayal with giving them the courage to are seeking for reconciliation with family members or to forgive folks that wronged them.

Roumie himself has emphasised that forgiveness is not continually easy — however it is important to the Christian life. He has spoken about the want to launch resentment and believe

CHAPTER 7

faith in action – persevering with Their Legacy

religion, when virtually lived, does no longer remain constrained to non-public revel in — it extends into movement, inspiring others and shaping groups. Jonathan Roumie and Takashi Nagai confirmed that authentic faith actions beyond perception and transforms into a life of service, forgiveness, and ethical courage. Their examples remind us that religion isn't always truly a supply of private power — it turns into a pressure for restoration, reconciliation, and fantastic exchange inside the global.

Jonathan Roumie's work as an actor and religious advise and Takashi Nagai's position as a health practitioner, writer, and peacebuilder replicate how faith, while translated into movement, will become a catalyst for wish and renewal. Their legacies venture us to remember how our very own religion can encourage motion — now not just in moments of disaster, but inside the normal alternatives that shape our relationships and communities. This chapter explores how Roumie and Nagai's religion-stimulated actions have left a long-lasting effect on the sector and the way their examples maintain to guide others towards deeper faith and meaningful carrier.

Jonathan Roumie's function within the chosen has opened doors no longer best for creative fulfillment but additionally for religious outreach and ministry. Roumie has embraced his platform as an possibility to share his religion publicly and encourage others to are looking for a deeper courting with God.

Roumie's portrayal of Jesus within the selected isn't clearly an artistic fulfillment — it is an act of spiritual provider. He has described his performance as an offering to God, rooted in prayer and private devotion. before filming each scene, Roumie regularly prays for guidance, asking God to apply him as an tool to mirror Christ's message authentically.

The emotional intensity and humanity he brings to the function have helped visitors have interaction with Christ's tale in a more personal and handy way. Roumie's Christ isn't distant or judgmental — he's compassionate, susceptible, and relational. This technique has resonated with audiences from various backgrounds, many of whom have shared that watching the selected helped them reconnect with their religion or heal from past wounds.

Roumie's commitment to accuracy and emotional honesty has made the selected one of the maximum successful religion-based media projects in history. Its international reach has turned Roumie right into a religious discern, with human beings from around the world seeking to him for steering and thought.

beyond his work on screen, Roumie has turn out to be a vocal advocate for Christian religion and values. He regularly speaks at religion-based activities, prayer gatherings, and meetings, in which he stocks his testimony of surrender and trust in God's plan.

Roumie's message emphasizes the importance of prayer, the sacraments, and believe in God's timing. He encourages younger people to peer religion now not as a set of regulations but as a non-public dating with Christ. His capability to connect with more youthful audiences has helped bridge the generational gap inside the Church and encourage a brand new wave of religious renewal. similarly to his public ministry, Roumie has used his platform to guide charitable causes. He has partnered with corporations that cope with troubles which include poverty, dependancy, and intellectual fitness. His message is apparent: religion isn't always just about private salvation — it is about serving others and dwelling out Christ's name to like each other.

Roumie's paintings has additionally had an ecumenical effect. the chosen has been embraced by Catholics, Protestants, and Orthodox Christians alike. Roumie's personal Catholic religion and his openness to running with Christians of different traditions replicate a spirit of harmony that transcends denominational divides.

Roumie regularly emphasizes that the message of the selected — God's love and mercy — is standard. His willingness to collaborate with Christians from distinctive backgrounds has contributed to a developing feel of shared motive and religious renewal across Christian groups.

Takashi Nagai's legacy of religion in action is rooted in his response to the devastation of Nagasaki. His willingness to serve others in spite of his personal struggling and his commitment to forgiveness inside the face of impossible loss remain powerful examples of the way faith can transform even the maximum tragic situations.

After surviving the atomic bombing of Nagasaki, Nagai selected to stay within the town and care for the wounded. no matter his personal radiation sickness and the lack of his wife, he labored tirelessly to treat the injured and luxury the loss of life.

Nagai's commitment to his clinical vocation reflected his knowledge of religion as carrier. He believed that his calling as a physician become no longer separate from his religion — it was an immediate expression of Christ's command to care for the struggling. His willingness to sacrifice his own fitness and comfort to serve others have become a source of desire for the shattered community of Nagasaki.

even as his health deteriorated, Nagai continued to write and talk approximately the need for forgiveness and reconciliation. His message turned into no longer one in every of political blame but of spiritual renewal. He challenged survivors to see the tragedy no longer as a reason for hatred but as an opportunity for moral awakening and peacebuilding.

one of Nagai's maximum radical acts of religion became his decision to forgive the ones accountable for the bombing of Nagasaki. At a time while many survivors were ate up by means of bitterness and rage, Nagai preached forgiveness as the course to restoration.

He considered the bombing as a form of redemptive suffering — a sacrifice that would lead to religious rebirth for Japan and the sector. His name for forgiveness changed into no longer an excuse for injustice, however a popularity that real recuperation may want to handiest be performed through reconciliation.

Nagai's writings, mainly The Bells of Nagasaki, became a ethical and religious guide for survivors and future generations. His capacity to look grace and motive even within the midst of destruction displays a profound faith in God's providence.

Nagai's legacy as a peace recommend extends past Nagasaki. His life and writings had been studied via historians, theologians, and peace activists as a version of ethical leadership in the face of violence. His message that peace calls for both justice and forgiveness continues to resonate in international dialogues approximately struggle resolution and reconciliation.

Nagai's tale has also encouraged the Catholic Church's coaching on conflict and peace. His witness reinforces the idea that peace isn't always genuinely the absence of struggle — it is the presence of justice, mercy, and mutual understanding.

though their lives have been separated by way of time and circumstance, Jonathan Roumie and Takashi Nagai share a commonplace legacy of faith in movement. Their lives demonstrate that true faith isn't always passive — it requires response and engagement with the arena.

Roumie's religion stimulated him to surrender his profession to God and use his achievement to carry others towards Christ. His portrayal of Jesus and his public ministry replicate a commitment to making Christ's message available and relatable. Nagai's religion empowered him to stand suffering with courage and to pick forgiveness over resentment. His clinical carrier, writings, and advocacy for peace stay lasting testaments to the power of faith in action.

both men mirror the reality that religion is not a guard from suffering — it's miles the energy to stand struggling with braveness and the grace to reply to injustice with mercy. Their tales undertaking us to don't forget how our very own faith can form our lives and influence the sector round us.

Jonathan Roumie and Takashi Nagai encompass the Christian call to stay out religion through service and forgiveness. Roumie's work in media and religious advocacy and Nagai's paintings as a physician and peacebuilder demonstrate that religion becomes maximum powerful whilst it actions beyond notion and becomes motion. Their legacies remind us that genuine religion isn't always measured by using words alone — it's miles measured by means of the willingness to love, serve, and forgive, even when it's far difficult. via their lives, we see that faith in motion has the energy to heal hearts, reconcile groups, and remodel the sector.

conclusion – United through faith and Resilience

faith and resilience are of the most powerful forces that form human lives, and the memories of Jonathan Roumie and Takashi Nagai show how these characteristics can encourage profound transformation even in the face of substantial challenges. even though they lived in exclusive times, confronted distinctive struggles, and expressed their faith in distinct methods, Roumie and Nagai are united by means of a shared commitment to dwelling out their faith with braveness, compassion, and forgiveness. Their lives screen that actual faith isn't always truely a remember of perception — it is a supply of electricity that empowers people to stand suffering, to heal wounds, and to inspire others towards deeper religion and reconciliation.

Jonathan Roumie's adventure displays the transformative electricity of surrender and trust in God's plan. His decision to give up manipulate and region his future in God's hands led to non-public and expert breakthroughs that handed his expectations. His portrayal of Jesus within the chosen has reached millions, supporting viewers hook up with Christ's message of love and mercy in a deeply personal way. Roumie's willingness to use his platform to propose for faith and ethical integrity has made him not best a a success actor however additionally a religious guide for many. His story teaches that religion, whilst absolutely embraced, turns into a source of innovative and religious power — able to breaking thru worry and doubt to show deeper reason.

Takashi Nagai's existence stands as a testomony to the electricity of religion within the face of unimaginable loss and suffering. As a survivor of the atomic bombing of Nagasaki, Nagai had every reason to succumb to bitterness and melancholy. as a substitute, he selected forgiveness and peace. His clinical provider to the wounded, his religious writings, and his call for reconciliation meditated a profound accept as true with in God's windfall. Nagai's choice to forgive the ones responsible for the destruction of his metropolis was now not an act of weak point — it turned into an act of ethical power. His legacy reminds us that forgiveness isn't forgetting or excusing injustice — it is selecting love over hatred and peace over revenge.

each Roumie and Nagai show that religion isn't about escaping suffering — it's far approximately finding energy and that means thru it. Roumie's faith gave him the braveness to persevere thru expert failure and uncertainty, leading to a leap forward that allowed him to inspire tens of millions thru his portrayal of Christ. Nagai's religion gave him the energy to stand the destruction of his home and the death of his wife with grace, and to transform his personal loss into a venture of recuperation and reconciliation for his human beings.

Their testimonies converge on a powerful truth: faith is not an summary notion — it's far a lived revel in that shapes how we reply to existence's greatest demanding situations. Roumie's artistic ministry and Nagai's scientific and ethical leadership replicate one-of-a-kind expressions of the equal non secular electricity — the strength to believe God's plan, to reply to suffering with braveness, and to select forgiveness over hatred.

The legacy of Jonathan Roumie and Takashi Nagai demanding situations us to do not forget how faith can form our personal lives. Roumie's message of trusting in God's plan and Nagai's instance of forgiving even the gravest injustices remind us that religion isn't always simplest about private salvation — it is approximately how we live in relationship with others. Their lives train us that religion and resilience are not separate features — they are deeply connected. authentic resilience comes from the conviction that even in struggling, God's presence remains.

In a global frequently marked through division, suffering, and struggle, the examples of Roumie and Nagai stand as beacons of wish and reconciliation. Roumie's ability to communicate Christ's message thru art and Nagai's willingness to reply to destruction with forgiveness remind us that faith has the energy to heal, unite, and transform. Their lives encourage us to see faith no longer as a passive safe haven however as an energetic force for top — a source of strength that enables us to stand adversity with grace and to respond to hatred with love.

in the end, Roumie and Nagai's stories monitor that faith and resilience are not character achievements — they're presents to be shared with the arena. Roumie's portrayal of Jesus continues to draw humans towards God, even as Nagai's writings and legacy retain to inspire movements for peace and reconciliation. Their lives remind us that real religion isn't always defined by using the absence of war — it is described by using the capability to face warfare with courage, to forgive whilst it is difficult, and to agree with that God's plan is extra than human knowledge.1

Jonathan Roumie and Takashi Nagai are united via a shared legacy of faith and resilience. Their lives mission us to encompass the identical strength and grace in our personal lives — to believe in God's plan even when the path is doubtful, to forgive even when it feels not possible, and to allow religion manual our actions in the direction of restoration and peace. through their witness, we are reminded that religion isn't clearly approximately notion — it's far approximately how we live, love, and serve others, even inside the face of life's best trials.

Made in the USA
Las Vegas, NV
23 March 2025